Visit us at
SequoiaKidsMedia.com
for bonus downloadable content

Written by Todd and Peggy Snow

Photographs © Shutterstock.com: pixfly; FeelplusCreator; Monkey Business; Lopolo; arrowsmith2; titov dmitriy; FocusDzign; Konstantin Ermakov; franz12; In The Light Photography; K1r1; all_about_people; fizkes; yurakrasil; vectorfusionart; VH-studio; Stephanie Zieber; Juliya Shangarey; Yuliya Evstratenko; Fedorova AA; Bangkok Click Studio; Alim Yakubov; Pranch; Krakenimages.com; EwaNew; Prostock-studio; Alonafoto; BELOWA IRINA; Lipatova Maryna; HAPPY-LUCKY; Sergey Novikov; sivivolk; Creative Minds2; madtom; HowLettery; Cosmic_Design; funbutterfly.

Published by Sequoia Kids Media,
an imprint of Sequoia Publishing & Media, LLC

Sequoia Publishing & Media, LLC,
a division of Phoenix International Publications, Inc.

8501 West Higgins Road, Chicago, Illinois 60631

Customer Service: CS@SequoiaKidsBooks.com

www.SequoiaKidsMedia.com

Library of Congress Control Number: 2022908701

ISBN 979-8-7654-0042-5

Mindfulness is a feeling of being aware.
It's focusing on what you do,
paying attention to your feelings,
and noticing the world around you.

Mindfulness is in you to listen. Keep your ears open and eyes on the speaker.

If you have a question quietly wait your turn.
Being mindful helps you understand and learn.

DID YOU KNOW?
Practicing mindfulness improves your ability to focus.

Mindfulness is in you
to notice how others feel.
Sometimes people are hurt or sad.

DID YOU KNOW?
Mindfulness develops empathy: the ability to understand another person's feelings.

Share kind words and a hug too.
It's important to be mindful of those around you.

Mindfulness is in you to know what's good for your body. Are you STRONG, flexible or fast on your feet?
FUN FACT:
Google allows employees to have daily mindful sessions.

Try sports, yoga, or dance to see what you can do well. By listening to your body, you'll be able to tell.

Mindfulness is in you to be safe when you play. Look around and notice what's going on.

Stay near an adult you know. Play safely and be mindful wherever you go.

Mindfulness is in you to pay attention to your thoughts. When something is hard, say...

I can do this!

FUN FACT:
Being mindful helps you be more creative.

Having positive thoughts is good for you. It can help you be better at what you do.

Mindfulness is in you to choose healthy foods. You get energy from eating vegetables and fruit.

A variety of healthy food is best for you. It's good for your mind and body too.

DID YOU KNOW?
Mindful eating helps digestion.

Mindfulness is in you to meditate.

Close your eyes and relax your face.

Breathe in and out as you count to ten.
Focus on your stomach and try it again.

DID YOU KNOW?
Mindfulness can improve sleep.

Mindfulness is in you to notice the beauty of nature.

Your senses let you enjoy the wonders of the world.

Do you hear birds chirping? Feel a cool breeze?
Do you see butterflies, wildflowers, and trees?

Mindfulness is in you to use kind words.
How do you feel when you have something to say?

Think before using your voice.
Being friendly is
always a good choice.

DID YOU KNOW? Mindfulness teaches the brain to think before reacting.

Mindfulness is in you to sense how you feel.
Are you happy or mad? Excited or sad?

When feelings confuse you, what can you do?

Talk to people who care about you.

Mindfulness is in you to help others in need.

You're capable of knowing what to do.

Look for ways to help and share.
Giving attention to others lets them know you care.

Mindfulness is in you to care for pets. They need attention and depend on people.

Is your dog hungry? Does your cat want to play? Be mindful of their needs so they're happy each day.

FUN FACT:
Animals are good examples of mindfulness because they naturally live in the present moment.

Mindfulness is in YOU!

Let it guide your thoughts and actions.

FUN FACT:
"Our life is shaped by our mind, for we become what we think."
—*Buddha*

Be present in each moment and all that you do.

It's what makes you uniquely YOU.

MINDFULNESS BOOSTERS

I will be mindful when others are speaking and give them my attention.

I will be mindful of how I feel and try to eat healthy and get exercise.

I will be mindful of my actions and treat others with respect.

I will be mindful when people or animals are in need and help them.

I will be mindful of my thoughts and think positively.

I will be mindful of nature and take time to enjoy it.